OF MAGIC AND PROFANITY

(BRAVING DEVOTION IN THE YEAR OF TWENTY-ONE)

SANSKRITI SODAI

INDIA • SINGAPORE • MALAYSIA

ISBN 979-8-89233-873-8

for

those who wander, and are lost perhaps,
who have homes in places not found on our maps,
who travel the roads paved with words and rhyme,
our worlds have magic, we live outside time.

Contents

Magic and Profanity

Poetry on your shelf that's been waiting to be read,
A cup of morning tea warm and cozy in your bed.
The ever-changing cloud pleads for your gaze, just a wee-
And watch itself morphed into your own tales of fantasy!

A flower growing through the gravel on some old, untrodden ways
Made all the way up just to bring a smile to your face.
And imagine! You walk right past it without a nod,
The smell of rain is missed on you, so is the thunder for applaud.

And who on earth would wish such trite, to live a life so tragic!
When each breath you take, in its own right, is such a work of magic.

Some Rights, Some Left.

A scheme with all minute details,
A life planned perfect to the 't',
The gains and losses it entails
You know with all certainty.

The rights you have to take to reach,
The destination on the map,
Sometimes, there's an inadvertent breach,
Some path is left to fill the gap.

And dusty, finally, you've come
To the dream you had once carved
Onto the pages of the tome
That is your life for which you've starved.

The book's now ready, come savour!
With fulfilled plans, pages are rife.
But still the mind awkwardly lingers
over
The blank pages, the unlived life.

trust
/trʌst/
NOUN
reliance on and confidence in
the truth, worth, reliability, etc. of a
person or thing.

faith
/feɪθ/
NOUN
strong or unshakeable belief in
something, especially without proof
or evidence.

Trust and Faith

Trust and faith, those treasures two
You keep them in the chest self-same.
And yet the keys to them, they do
Exist apart, bear different names.

I know who I am, to earn
The trust unlocked, made yours
some day.
But will the faith too have its turn?
It is not for me to say.

Its value sits too high for me
To earn in this one life I live.
You yourself will forge that key,
It was never mine to give.

Eyes

There are eyes that shift hither-thither
You struggle to catch their hold.
There are gazes that smoothly slither
Up on you, unafraid and bold.

There is always a shy pair
Stealing their momentary glances.
Always looking to rest somewhere
They don't have to meet others' advances.

There are the playful eyes that never halt,
You see through a kaleidoscope.
It's like they've locked in them spherical vaults
Rays of joy and mirth and hope.

There are the deeper ones that when they look,
They stare into your soul, their pleasure.

You feel unclothed, an open book
That they peruse at their own leisure.

There are the eyes that when
I see into them I feel they're pools
Of clear water, oozing over the ends.
They well up easily, such fools.

And then there are the pair
Of the most beautiful eyes I've seen.
You can in them, endlessly stare
And bask in their moon-like sheen.
You feel blessed to hold a second's gaze.
It's like they're art drawn by a power profound.
And yet they remain still, no faze
Knowing the Immaculate that in them I found.
And I said they're art, and rightly so
For in them I find what I want to know
I fear it matters not what lies behind
I'll continue to find in them, what I want to find.

A Drop of Dew

As heavy mist subsides, and my sole feel frigid ground,
The eastern eye, cloud-robed, too has begun its diurnal round.
But I walk not on heat-hardened hay, or cold withered flowers
My path I see- green firmament, grass laden with shimmering stars.
The cool, it at first stings, then gently blankets me in haze,
Feel winter's warm hug, and as I slowly shift my gaze
To a drop, a penny-pool lapped on the leaf outgrowing the hedge,
And it seemed the blade bore bravely the whole Tethys on its edge.
My eyes pass over dianthus, but wait, its tiny petals are
With Baker's sugar-sweet sprinkled, just like his fresh-made Linzer Tarts.
Is it this powdery nectar that beckons to the bee?

I forgot it was just water poured from nature's brewery.
How wonderful, the scenes that the eyes can conjure in lieu
Of the pearl that nature grows sans shell- that is a drop of dew.

Some Sins

I pray my soul be sheltered from pride,
May it know the transience where it doth reside.
May I drown in shame ere envy takes birth,
Rest assured in my own, or even its lack of worth.
Be saved from my own, and the other as well,
Know that love only asks, it'll wait, never compel.
The world can do better with some restrain,
A firm hand refusing to cede wrath all the reins.
May I drink from my cup and sit back content
It drives me to a slumber before greed finds a vent.
There's gluttony, I have to write about it a lot,
For now, I sleep, I've had too much food for thought.

Verse I

When you're slipping off the edge, I doubt
Who would you rather let know-
A thousand hands rushing to pull you out
Or one that never let go?

Strife

Tell me more of tales so grand,
Of timeless battles in a distant land,
Of strength and valour, and hard-fought glory
The blood soaked forever in the fabric of a story.

When the shaking hands sounded the horn,
Spirits united, and bodies torn.
The rapture of war-cry, fading to a hum
Of death drifting over the unfortunate some.

The hand that holds the sceptre in a vise
Cares only for its jewel, the weight it'll despise.
It'll strike it down with the fury of Gods

On the man it'll kill to his kin's applauds.

And the men still march with a swelling pride
To drumbeats ringing death closer with each stride.
Hands torn apart by the sword of the foe
Will still count as masons of the foundations they'll sow

Of an empire built high on the mounds
Of the umpteen souls free from the hounds
That bark, to set them alight to give warm sighs
To a hearth whose smoke frees from the turrets kissing the skies.

The castle that once made the sky overcast,
Now slumbers in its ruins, resting in the past.

Not blood-drunk verdure, but cement and steel
Sprawls all around, we no more kneel.

Or maybe 'tis an adage as old as the tale
That it gets repeated every epoch without fail-
I know not whether it's in words or ways
This time; the hand may be buried but the sceptre stays?

Regardless of the hand pulling the threads,
This freedom, unprecedented, onward treads.
There's still cold, and the embers call,
To warm just a bit, for a moment to stall.

But prithee, tell me, is there ever rcst so unruffled?-
Walls so high, you never see scuffle?

But now we can together touch the skies and beyond
Build a tower of Babel on an ever stronger bond.

I'm warm in my bed, behind my walls high,
But I don't fear the cold, the wrath of the sky.
Come, with me, we ask to be blessed with life.
Our swords are sheathed, but we pray for strife.

p.s. It goes without saying, but the meaning of the word 'strife' which carries the whole poem is the one that means 'earnest endeavour'. Any other negative connotation of the same does not convey my intent.

THE EXPL RERS

From Dehra to Mussoorie

Under the rich tapestry
Of a coal black sky,
We start our slow ascend
Up the mountains ever high.
The majesty of the mountains-
It's a beauty so grand,
There's a peace it quietly houses
In its lush, snowy upland.

You drive up the tar road,
As it goes round and round-
A serpent coiling in its lap
The jewel it somehow found.
The winds slowly turn cool,
And cooler they turn still
As you go on in your journey
On the road climbing uphill.

And right when you're prepared
To sit back and rest a while,
Just feel the cold gushes
On your drowsy, sleepy smile-
Your face drops to your left,
But what is left is not a town asleep-
It's a spectacle of life and light
Switched on when the slope came steep.

A myriad glowing lights afloat
In the quiet depths of the valley,
A constellation of stars
Not in the sky but down the alley
Of the sleepy town you left behind
When dusk quickly approached,
But much to your awe, it housed
So many flames now stoked-

And they look like tiny lamps
From the heights, now so afar,
Like lamps floating in a pond
You're slowly circling in your car.
The sight is right divine,

You circumscribe the skies so dreamy.
Perhaps this divinity is why
This land is called Devbhoomi.

And just as you rest back
To bask in the silent beauty,
It starts to blur away
The sight turns back sooty.
You close your eyes and hope
The picture stays- you saved the best stills.
But just as you prepare to rest,
You're woken to fog, you've reached the Queen of Hills.

Comforting Cold, Relentless Warmth

There's a flutter in my stomach
That starts to rise in a whirl,
Like butterflies in a flummox
Who laid trapped, suddenly unfurl.

There's a warmth that it encases;
I feel it slowly blanket my insides
Like approaching summer melting icy glazes
Of the long winter- that in me resides.

I actually like the cold weather,
Feel snug in its sleepy cocoon.
But now I see there's space for another,
My home can have one more room.

The warmth, the swirl of things unknown,
They have reached my neck, now my mouth;
They long to be let out and be blown
Onto the wind- free, untamed, even uncouth.

But the only channel I know of
Is of ink as it reaches for the nib of my pen.
The summer has to let go off
Its wilderness, as I lock it in my diary, page ten.

Maybe, today, if I leave the page be.
And the pen- in my pocket I place.
Tomorrow it'll fall out, and he'll pick, hand it to me
And I can finally say a 'hello' to fill yesterday's space.

Brown Eyes

Like coffee brewed at break of day,
Soft-swirling, simmering to a bulge,
The longer that you make it stay
The sharper when you at last indulge.

It's honey dripping like velvet
Hugging its vessel close.
Its sweet trail will beget
All those thirsty to its shores.

You'd get heavily drunk on the caramel
That glistens when sunrays embrace it from the skies,
You want to pause just a moment, to breathe, but oh well
You're already drowning in those damning brown eyes.

Verse II

Yes my dreams are big, they're bright,
My ambition stands too tall.
My destination's far, barely within sight
Back in my room, I need to crawl.

But a justification, I find hard to heave,
For the busy race our lives feign..
Saving my steps, one short of a crusty autumn leaf,
Not a breath to spare for the smell of the rain.

Innocence

Starry eyes, filled with wonder
They see the world untainted.
No reality dares to tear asunder
The perfect dream they've painted.

I leapt among the clouds untamed
My own flag waving high.
No burden in this world I claimed,
I'm light as wind, rising up the sky.

And then, one day you run up the lease,
The din's too loud to silence.
The music in your ears long ceased,
There's only screams of violence.

You'll know the world for what it has been,
You'll see yourself clearer too.
There's only darkness to be seen
Outside, and inside you.

It's all-engulfing, I feel lost,
It's how this always goes then?
A child grown up, will know the cost
Of tasting the fruit of Eden.

I want to be a bird once more,
Fly up the blues, up high.
Swim far into the sea; the shore
In my sight now always lies.

To my snow-globe world, I want return,
That I can switch on at night.
The glow warms me, the world too yearn
Maybe, for a small light.

Verse III

And when I sigh the day's now over,
My ambitions and vision on the side table I lower,
Take off my glasses to a blur of my dream...
A book and blanket by the fireplace, coffee with extra cream.

Shooting Star

Oh, shooting star, what wishes be
Made upon you all these years?
The love and longing thrust on thee,
You're made guard against all fears.

Much like the wish I make on your fall-
The promise of love for which I yearn,
You smile..light up my skies, you stall,
And on you go, never to return.

Forgettance

The vivid portrait in my mind
Is fading in a blur.
I'm glad for it to be so kind
To forget all, as it were.

A voice I heard as clear as day,
I now see slowly soften
To a hazy whisper that fogs my way
In the streets I visited often.

'Good riddance, of remembrance'- I sigh.
It's of relief, I must say.
'Why get anchored down?'- I lie
down, free of burdens that held any sway.

My heart still skips a beat though
At the sight of those unposted letters.
So I fold them up, and inside they go
Of my drawer, -their permanent fetters.

The poems in them never saw light
Of eyes for which they were born.
There's an ache in my heart, it might
Be just the poet, whose words got torn.

There's nothing I feel, nothing wrong.
But for folded paper, tucked away for that long
A slight peek, a little tug is all it takes to start
To tear at the folds, come apart.

I Choose Surfeit

The thirsty looks for every drop
That neither quenches nor lets you die.
You run and crawl to the final stop,
Every moment of anguish, for which you vie.

There's pain and grief and fleeting laughter,
Are the tears of joy or of loss are they?
You forget, but does it matter after
The moment's passed, and what of it stays?

Is there a key that can lock away
All the gloom of this world and some more of mine?
The scales of my justice, no burden they weigh.
At that altar of beneficence, can I get a morsel to dine?

I fear there's not a bite left with Thee
For me, or for much poorer souls of this earth.
I care not what will be left of me,
Only what stands now, with no claim to any worth.

I come with no wish or woe or will
There's nothing I brought, nothing my hands can carry uphill.
This empty, hollow life can house nothing but love. Absolute.
I'll hold it with a smile, protect it with arms resolute.
And if it too escapes me, I will thank it for that while.
I'll choose warm tears to hug my face any day over a parched smile.

I'll Write My Love for You in Sand

I'll write my love for you in sand,
And watch it, by the waves erased.
The world forgets, but will my hand
Lose touch of all the words it traced?

In stone that turns to dust with time
How can I carve that you are mine?
And so I let the ocean take
My words for you, for their own sake.

And in those depths they'll always live
Sometimes the wind, a hand may give
And bring them up in feral waves,
No love of mine, a homage craves.

Go try- efface, defile, go kill
My words, they will live on until
The day the wanton wind stands still,
They'll last as long as the oceans will.

To Him Who I've Yet to Find

I may not know my love of yet,
But I know the heart I seek.
My pen when on the page I set,
It knows the soul of whom I speak.

Two souls entwined, yet apart persisting
Hearts beating in tandem
A romance with no end existing
Oh! To love with reckless abandon.

A Girl Born

She was unwanted before she was born,
Her birth rang bells of worries for her kin,
Every breath she drew invited scorn
It seemed her very existence was a protracted sin.

She will be, to her brother, constantly compared.
Or worse- be ignored and forgotten she will
They sent her brother to school, for him they cared
While she was forced into 'her' job of household drivel.

They fed the brother well, they bought him books,
Said they didn't have enough to afford her the same

They tell her to be docile, and focus on her looks
Because that's how they'll buy her a groom worth the name.

They slowly kill her freewill, say- "Girls have no vocation."
She'll always need the hero to save her in the story
Each penny they saved, at the cost of her education,
They bundle up and give in a big, fat dowry.

From the moment she opened her eyes, they had said-
"We're doomed, our family's fate is ill-ridden"
They fettered her in chains, anchored down her rising head
And then conveniently proceeded to call her the burden.

But they don't know of the immensity of her dreams,
The intensity of her will, the passion in her eyes.
She will carve a boat to manoeuvre this tempestuous stream
She'll grow her own wings to conquer the skies.

And yet, this is the story of the 'lucky' ilk,
Who find themselves existing through all the pain.
Countless were killed in the womb, or drowned in milk,
By the same hands whose blood they carry in their veins.

'Save Girl Child'-we all exclaim !
But let the girl 'live' is what we often forget and refute
Her life comes not from an existence in chains,
But what her empowered self, to this world will contribute !

Basking, Slumbering, Saffron Dusk.

Tenth day. New office. I was travelling back from work
When the same auto-driver decided to give me a ride.
I lowered my head to nod, his gaze slightly lurked
But then nodded back, as I quickly sat by his side.

The back was as always stuffed
With almost the same faces I see each day-
Silent, or if they'd been together long enough
Conversing, searching for the next thing to say.

"Brother, now, if not us, then who could
Preserve this country, protect our faith?"
-announced a man, hoping we all would
Look up and take part in his debate.

"In the name of secularism, we are stumbling!
We're breaking the foundations of our religion!
Do you want to see this country crumbling?
Or the unified nation that we envision?"

"Unified indeed"- I said in a hush
And realised the driver's gaze shift towards me.
"I knew it brother, you were one of us-
Who realise the danger looming over the country."

"No, but the unity.."- I tried making my case
"Even among us, it's felt by only few"- he cut in.
And then ostensibly wiped the sweat off his face
With the saffron scarf he was wearing.

"No we have to unify, support each other"-

"Precisely son !"- the man sitting behind rejoiced.
But before I continue without interruption any further,
Came my destination, silencing my voice.

"All of us together have to stand unified"
"We need each other for a cause like this!"
Perhaps if they'd heard me, they wouldn't be so surprised
When I replied to their goodbye with a 'Khuda Hafiz'.

"Hamid! You just came back too?"
Said a cheerful Jyoti at the door.
"Are these new ones also harassing you?"
She pestered, for me to reveal more.

It didn't take her long to discern
The somewhat familiar silence on my face
As she continued to comfort me amid her concern-

"Don't you dare fall victim to this communal craze!"

I did not have the heart to tell her
It's her who they were calling a victim
Of an agenda I was apparently promoting,
By marrying my Jyoti, when I was a Muslim.

My thoughts were paused as Abeer flung onto my lap
The ray of light I saw at each day's end
And started pandering me with his umpteen questions,
Questions whose answers I could easily lend.

Until…

Until he asked me "Who am I?"
And I wanted to answer-"To this world you are a boon."
But I knew today his existence was diminished to stats that cried-
"Muslims are going to overtake India…soon."

A Tree Contemplating

Standing in the woods alone,
There's a tall and mighty tree,
And all these years since it was sown,
It's been showering love for free.

It houses squirrels and a myriad birds,
Their families call it home.
Its canopy gives shade to the herds
Of cattle on a wayward roam.

It gives life and living
To all who come and plead.
It's spent its life in giving
All that could sprout from a tiny seed.

And standing now for all these years
Its shadow too felt grand.
It's towering over all its peers,
Could embrace them all in a single hand.

It hears the evening chirping ranks,
The songs sung to its beauty.
Serenaded a note of thanks
By the larks perching on duty.

And winters came and winters went
And it kept standing tall.
No storm could make that trunk o'rbent,
It stood to answer every call.

And when it thought it'd done enough
It prepared to wither in peace someday,
Came a storm, so cruel, so rough,
Its mighty trunk began to sway.

And down it went, and downer still
And its head for once touched grass
And more, then more it laid down till,
It was one with the marsh.

And in a single jerk it broke,
It laid down, now at rest
For all time to come, no one to stroke
It where it bore its fruit the best.

As night approached, it saw the forest,
And the realisation's been whetting..
You cast your shadow the tallest
When the sun is slowly setting.

And the voices toy, they don't spare,
They fable -"If a tree will fall
In the forest, but no one's there to hear,
Does it make a sound or not at all?"

It matters not what's being said,
The tree gave all that it could
Till it ran out and was struck dead,
It merged right back into where it stood.

But contemplating, as it often did
The tree wondered, if on hitting the ground,
The voices would even recognize his,
If in fact, it made a sound?

Fin

And then the ink runs dry,
The tea is out, it's late,
No clouds above, a clear sky,
I'm just looking for some shade.

I know they axed down the trees
The scars on earth run deep,
Maybe, I sow just one seed,
Look after its upkeep.

And one day, in its shade I'll lie,
Or maybe someone else will,
See the clouds pass leisurely by
And know that magic resides here still.

About the Author

Sanskriti Sodai is a twenty-one year old writer from India. She has been writing poems and short stories since she was in class fourth. Literature for her has always been both an escape from reality as well as a mould for it. This, you'll find reflected in her works, as they seek to make poetry out of both- the silent beauties of life as well as the harsh realities of it. Magic and Profanity is her first published collection of poems.

www.ingramcontent.com/pod-product-compliance
Lightning Source LLC
LaVergne TN
LVHW090139160826
845673LV00017B/2521

* 9 7 9 8 8 9 2 3 3 8 7 3 8 *